How to Be Destroy Lo

Written by: Beau Norton

CEO & Founder of Health & Happiness Foundation

Self-confidence is a quality one must possess if he or she wishes to be happy and fulfilled. Self-doubt is the killer of all dreams. It can creep in without being noticed, and from there it wreaks havoc on almost every area of our lives. In this guide, I will show you the strategies I used to defeat my demons of self-doubt and go from a shy, insecure kid to someone who lives confidently and believes in no limits...

Chapter 1: Power of Positivity

"You cannot tailor-make the situations in life, but you can tailor-make the attitudes to fit those situations."

-Zig Ziglar

Making any kind of positive change in life requires a positive mindset. Negative thinking patterns will prevent you from doing many of the things that you need to do in order to build the extreme confidence that is required to live the life of your dreams. In fact, negative thinking is the absolute opposite of confidence. To build the inner confidence that you desire, you must learn to be optimistic, hopeful, and full of positive energy. In this chapter, I will show you how to cultivate the mindset of a confident, happy, and successful person.

Awareness & Thought Restructuring

The first step to creating a more positive mindset is to become aware of the nature of your thoughts. The majority of people go through their lives without ever taking the time to notice and analyze their own thoughts. It is a very common thing for people to go through life on autopilot and make very few conscious decisions, however, this is not their fault. The mind has great power and momentum. If you do not learn to control your own thinking processes, you will have very little control over your life and the decisions you make. Your brain will tend to take over and make all the decisions for you, but this is not always a good thing. Exercising more control over your life starts with awareness. I will now teach you a method that you can use to become more aware of your thoughts. Do this every day, and you will gradually become more capable of consciously creating the life that you desire.

Find a quiet spot where you can relax and be alone. Sit in a comfortable position, close your eyes, and just breathe. As you sit there and breathe, notice the thoughts that come into your mind. Pay extra attention to the types of thoughts you are having. Are you thinking of the past or the future? Do any of your thoughts make you feel anxious, depressed, angry, or any other kind of negative emotion? If you have negative thoughts of any kind pop into your head, write them down. If you do this every day, over time you will see yourself becoming more and more conscious of your thoughts throughout the day. As you become more aware of your thoughts, you will be able to replace the negative ones with positive ones that help you become more confident and capable of improving yourself in all areas of your life. Sit in silence for at least 10 minutes every day while focusing on your breath and noticing the thoughts that come to your mind. This is essential if you want to effectively create a positive attitude and gain control over your thoughts and actions.

Now, I will briefly discuss how to replace a negative thought with a positive one. As you get better and better at noticing and analyzing your own thoughts, you may get sudden insights at random times throughout the day that you never did previously. You may suddenly see very clearly the thoughts that you have in certain situations. You will likely catch yourself in the middle of thoughts that are in some way negative, and you will see how they are effecting your attitude and emotions. This is a very good sign. It means that you are creating more awareness in your life.

The moment you notice a negative thought come into your mind, immediately replace it with a positive one. For example, you think to yourself "I can't do this. I'm just not good enough." When you recognize it, immediately think to yourself, "delete" and then repeat back to yourself something like this three times: "Actually, I *can* do this, I just need to put in a little more effort." At first, your mind will not want to accept this new statement, because it is accustomed to more negative thought inputs. This is perfectly fine, because this thought restructuring exercise is meant to reprogram your mind over time. If you repeat a positive thought three times after every one negative thought, you tell your subconscious that the positive thought should be accepted instead. Slowly, your mind will adjust and begin to generate more positive thoughts. These thoughts will give you a more optimistic outlook on life, which is a necessary ingredient for positive change. The more you do this thought exercise, the more momentum you will gain in the direction of an extremely positive mindset, which is essential for building and maintaining true confidence.

"Optimism is the most important human trait, because it allows us to evolve our ideas, to improve our situation, and to hope for a better tomorrow."

- Seth Godin

Outside Influence

Restructuring your thoughts is an essential step in building a robust inner environment, but the outside world has the ability to come in and wipe out that inner strength if you aren't careful. Many of the thoughts that we have on a daily basis, whether positive or negative, are largely a result of the type of environment we are in most often. Take for example a kid that was raised by an abusive parent who always told him how worthless he was, or a kid who was bullied his whole life. These are two example of people raised in a negative environment with very little or no positive outside influence. Do you think these two people would have a positive outlook on life? It's possible, but unlikely. Environment is everything. To build extreme inner confidence, you must make an effort to surround yourself with positive people that think highly of you and encourage you often. This is not always easy in the world we live in, but it is crucial that you consciously decide to seek out a more positive environment for yourself.

Creating a positive environment sometimes means eliminating people from your life. From personal experience, I can say that this is the most difficult but rewarding part of the journey. It may not always be possible to eliminate the negative people from your life completely, such as in the case of those people being family members or people you live with, but it is important that you reduce the amount of time you spend with people that radiate negative energy.

If you have a certain friend or family member that seems to always doubt or criticize you in some way, tell them politely that you are trying to make positive changes in your life and would appreciate it if they would encourage your or say nothing at all. It is likely that they will get the hint and start to change their attitude towards you, but it is also possible they will begin to resent you for speaking out against them. The way people react will vary greatly, but if they react with more negativity, consider drastically reducing the amount of time you spend with them or cutting them out of your life completely. This can be a difficult process, but remember, optimism and positive energy in massive quantities is required for you to achieve the extreme confidence, success, and peace of mind that you desire. Anyone who drains you of that positive energy is directly interfering with the process of you becoming that person.

It has been said many times by many successful people that you are the average of the five people you spend the most time with. I have found this to be absolutely true. I cannot stress enough the importance of choosing who you spend your time with wisely. The people you interact with are constantly giving off a certain type of energy that directly affects your own energy. Thoughts and emotions are things. When someone has negative thoughts or emotions, they radiate from them as a form of physical energy that directly affects those around them. Choose your friends wisely so that you are always surrounded with positive energy. Choose friends that possess the qualities you wish to have. You will be inspired and motivated by them to become a stronger version of yourself.

Practice cultivating inner confidence by restructuring your thoughts, but also have the awareness to shape your outer environment in a way that supports you. Master your inner *and* outer environment, and you will guarantee your own success.

I would like to conclude this chapter with a quote by Gordon B. Hinckley that I found very fitting.

"What I am suggesting is that each of us turn from the negativism that permeates our society and look for the remarkable good among those with whom we associate, that we speak of one another's virtues more than we speak of one another's faults, that optimism replace pessimism, that our faith exceed our fears. When I was a young man and was prone to speak critically, my father would say: "Cynics do not contribute, skeptics do not create, doubters do not achieve."

Chapter 2: Fake It 'til You Make It

"Our bodies are apt to be our autobiographies."

-Frank Gillette Burgess

I'm sure you've heard the phrase, but can you really make something real by faking it? This is something I have been experimenting with for quite some time now, and I've concluded that this is a very powerful concept that has the ability to transform many lives if used properly. However, I've also realized that it is not enough to simply "fake it." In order to make lasting changes to your emotional state (feelings of confidence, happiness, etc.) you must learn to identify with what you are faking. In other words, you must *believe* in the emotion or quality you wish to possess and completely forget that you are faking it. More on this later, but for now I would like to discuss the basics of "faking it 'til you make it."

My idea of "faking it" has a lot to do with body language and the way one carries themself. Picture in your mind two people – one who is extremely confident and successful and one who is shy, awkward, and insecure. Now compare the body language of these two people. Which one stands up straight? Which one slouches? Which one walks with a pep in their step, and which one drags their feet? I'm sure you get the idea, but how can you use this knowledge to your advantage? The answer is simple: Emulate the person who possesses the qualities that you wish to possess. In this case, I am speaking specifically of body language. If you want to *feel* confident, you must learn to *act* confident. Use the following tips to improve your body language so that you can feel more confident:

Take long strides when you walk. Walk slightly faster than normal and act like you know where you're going. Look straight forward or slightly above eye level. Don't look at the ground.

When sitting down, sit up straight with a slight arch in your lower back. Keep your shoulders back and relaxed.

When standing, keep your arms relaxed and down at your sides. Don't put your hands in your pockets or fidget with anything.

When having a conversation, look the person directly in the eyes and maintain eye contact. If you are a man, and you meet eyes with a beautiful woman, do not look away until she does.

Speak loudly and clearly in conversations with others. Don't mumble.

I highly recommend that you do some type of exercise that strengthens your lower back. The best exercise for this is deadlifts. By strengthening your lower back, you make it far easier to sit up

straight and maintain good posture.
Exercise in general is great for improving
your posture as well as your self-image.

Practice positive body language while
going through your day. Take notice of
how you walk, talk, sit, stand, and interact
with others. When you become aware of
poor body language, immediately adjust it
to that of a more confident person. Do this
consistently and your new way of
behaving will become more and more
natural. You may even get some
compliments on the way you carry
yourself. You will be a changed person,
and people will take notice. You will have
effectively used your body to change your
mind. How is this possible?

The insecure person has poor posture and
weak body language because their
thoughts are negative and self-defeating.
The confident person's thoughts are
positive and self-empowering. In most
cases, it is the thought process of the
person that affects the way they carry

themselves, however, the reverse can be true as well. The mind-body connection is what allows you to directly affect your thoughts using your body language, and this is why "faking it until you make it" actually works. Carrying yourself in a confident way, even if you aren't confident at all, will make you feel at least slightly more confident. However, to have extreme confidence, you must be able to use the power of the body *and* the mind.

The power of thought restructuring combined with the power of positive body language will shoot your confidence through the roof! You can have an extremely positive mindset, but if you naturally have bad posture or body language, then you will not experience the highest levels of inner confidence that are possible for you. Similarly, poor thinking habits cannot be completely overridden by positive body language. Use the thought restructuring methods mentioned in the first chapter along with the tips in this chapter to cultivate confidence quickly.

Confidence and being happy go hand-in-hand. It is difficult to have one without the other, so taking steps to become a happier person will make becoming confident that much easier. The "fake it 'til you make it" approach can be applied to happiness also. All you have to do is fake a smile, and you will instantly feel a little happier. Smile at everyone you meet, even if you are having a bad day. You will give your subconscious mind the message to feel happy, and so you don't really need any reason at all to feel that way. Happiness is indeed a choice.

You Can Be Whoever You Want To Be

Remember, you always have the choice to consciously emulate the characteristics of the people you wish to be like. This essentially mean that you have the ability to become whoever you want if you have the right knowledge and skills to do so. If you use the strategies and techniques in this book and practice them regularly, you will gain the ability to shape your life and personality into whatever you choose. Remember though, this is not about trying to be someone else or create a false identity. It is about consciously choosing your own destiny and becoming the strongest version of yourself.

On a final note, I would like to briefly discuss the power of belief. The above methods will help you to feel much more confident and capable, but for lasting to change to occur, you must *believe* with conviction that you are a confident person. It is time to let go of the limiting beliefs that have been holding you back. One of the most profound truths is that we are what we believe ourselves to be. Forget what you've been told by your parents or friends. You have the ability to shape your own reality through the power of belief. Believe you are capable of extraordinary things and you will surely go on to achieve all that you desire to achieve. It's not enough to say it. You have to believe with all your heart that you are an amazing person who is capable of absolutely anything. You no longer have room for negativity in your life. Others will no longer bring you down. Greatness lies within you. Believe in yourself. Choose who you want to become, and then go be that person.

Here is a great book that explains everything you need to know about body language and how to carry yourself confidently:

The Definitive Guide of Body Language by Barbara and Allan Pease

Chapter 3: Goal Setting & Visualization

"Our plans miscarry because they have no aim. When a man does not know what harbor he is making for, no wind is the right wind."

-Seneca

Making steady progress in life is a fail-proof way to steadily increase your confidence, and the best way to ensure that you make progress is to set measurable goals for yourself and visualize the outcomes you would like to see. Without specific goals, you have nothing to aim for; with nothing to aim for, you have no way to measure your progress. In this chapter, I will share with you the goal setting and visualization strategies that countless successful people have used to achieve great things and drastically increase their self-confidence.

There was a time in my life when I felt very lost and unsure of myself, and I am willing to bet you know exactly how this feels. Most of us go through it at some point in our lives, but some people spend their whole lives feeling lost. I believe the main reason for this is because very few people have a grand vision for their life or a clearly defined purpose. I think that having extreme confidence requires one to have specific goals that they work towards every single day. Without something to work for, self-confidence dwindles and one's life can begin to feel dull and pointless. The truth is, confident people feel as if their life has meaning. Creating a grand vision for yourself and setting big goals will give your life plenty of meaning, and if you work towards those goals with your purpose in mind, your confidence will grow steadily along with your success. Now, let's explore some of the ways for you to discover your purpose in life and begin on the path to great achievement.

Program Your Subconscious Mind

Writing down your goals is the fastest way to achieve them, because it programs your subconscious mind to begin looking for ways to reach your desired destination. The more often you reprogram your goals into your subconscious mind by either writing them down or visualizing them, the stronger your desire and willpower will become. These are two essential ingredients for success. Having big goals that are compelling will make you more likely to want to achieve them. Desire and willpower simply cannot be created if you have goals that don't excite you.

If you don't have any major goals for yourself, well now is your time to make some. Whether or not you believe you can achieve your goals is not important right now. The important thing is that you set your goals high and you write them down without questioning them. If you could do or be anything in the world, what would it be? No matter how far-fetched it might sound, just simply write it down. Now I want you to go into great detail and write down exactly what your life would be like if you had already achieved your goal. This is where the visualization comes into play. Close your eyes and imagine yourself living your dreams. What would your life look like? Who would you see? What would you do? What would you smell, taste, feel, and so on? Use the power of your imagination and go to the place in the future where your life is absolutely incredible. Now begin writing down every detail of this scene in your mind. Just continue writing for 20 minutes or until you feel as if what you've written perfectly describes every detail of your ideal life. We'll call this your "dream sheet." This is a powerful exercise that will change your life in ways you couldn't imagine. Never underestimate the power of the subconscious mind.

Now that you have a detailed description of your ideal life, you can begin to program this image into your subconscious mind so that you will naturally be led in the direction of your dreams. The subconscious mind does not know the difference between what is real and what is imagined, so by visualizing on a consistent basis how you wish your life to be, you make it almost inevitable that you will turn that dream into reality. This is a powerful concept that should not be taken lightly. I have personally studied many successful people and have found that many of them attribute their success to the power of goal setting and visualization. These extremely successful people didn't always have high self-esteem and confidence. They had to build it over time and first visualize themselves as confident and capable people. Your confidence will increase as your goal becomes more clear and attainable. The way to make this happen is by consistently imagining yourself as a confident and successful person. Remember, the subconscious mind doesn't know what is real. Use the power of your imagination to create your reality.

Take the "dream sheet" that you created and read it to yourself at least twice per day. Even better, record yourself reading your dream sheet and listen to it on your mp3 player. As you are reading or listening to it, try to picture every detail in your mind. See where you will live and the people you will be with. Hear the conversations you will have and the sounds in your environment. Taste the food you will eat. Smell the fresh air. Feel what it feels like to be the confident, successful person you are destined to become. Read this sheet every day and practice visualizing it. Visualize it every spare second you get. Your dream may seem unattainable when you begin doing this, but the more you read your dream sheet and visualize your idea of a perfect life, the more you will believe in your ability to actually live those dreams. Of course, action will be required at some point if you wish to achieve your goals and drastically increase your confidence, but writing those goals down and seeing what your life will be like once you accomplish them is the first step and will make taking action so much easier.

Baby Steps to Success

So now you have some big dreams to inspire and motivate you, but how do you begin to make those dreams a reality when you lack the confidence to take the massive action that is required? Firstly, don't get overwhelmed by the large vision you have created for yourself. Simply visualize it on a daily basis to program it into your mind. Everything will come more naturally if you do this. At some point, you will need to take action if you plan on becoming an extremely confident person. Confidence is easily increased when you have a series of many small successes. With each success, you will become more confident in your ability to push your limits and do greater things, but you must start out at a level that is within your comfort zone.

Set yourself small daily and weekly goals that are steps towards your grand vision. Make sure that these small goals are attainable. They can be as simple as reading for 30 minutes or taking a walk, but it is important that you follow through and do them every day. If you set goals and fail to achieve them, it can actually lower your confidence, so that is why you need to start out with something that you *know* you can do. Write these small goals down somewhere and check them off your list every time you complete one. Every time you cross one of the goals off your list, you will experience a small boost in your confidence. A series of small things done over time lead to big results. As you see your life improving steadily, you will be more motivated to try things that are a little more difficult. Your confidence will grow with every small success, and you will come closer and closer to your grand vision.

Confidence is a result of progress, and that is why goal setting is so important. Goals will give you something to work towards and will give your life more meaning. You will begin to see that you are actually capable of more than you previously thought, and you will likely begin to wonder how far you can go. Keep the vision of your dreams in mind, set small goals that lead you there, and success and confidence will come naturally.

Brian Tracy is a goal setting and visualization expert. I highly recommend you check out his website here: BrianTracy.com

Chapter 4: Study Success

"Learning is acquired by reading books, but the much more necessary learning, the knowledge of the world, is only to be acquired by reading men, and studying all the various facets of them."

-Lord Chesterfield

If I had to attribute my growth as a human being to one thing, it would be my relentless study of successful people. I like to say often, "If you want to be the best, learn from the best." There is a vast amount to be learned from the people that have already done what we desire to do. Successful people in all walks of life have documented their knowledge and wisdom, and much of that information is readily available to us in the blink of an eye. The internet is an incredible blessing, especially for those who want to improve their lives. Let me take you through a few of the ways that you can begin using the internet and books to skyrocket your confidence and begin believing in your ability to achieve great things.

Autobiographies and Self-Help

Reading is great for so many reasons, but the main reason I recommend it is because it gives you the opportunity to learn from the greats that have come before you. Reading an autobiography of someone you admire can give you great insights into your own life and give you a different perspective on things. It can also help to reassure you that you're not alone in your struggles. Most successful people had to undergo lots of pain and suffering before they reached their greatest successes. Reading about people who came from humble beginnings and went on to achieve great things can give you a major confidence boost, because you will realize that greatness is not just for the privileged or lucky – greatness is for those who never give up and continue on in the face of resistance. If you are reading this right now, then you are on the right track. It shows that you haven't given up and are making an effort to improve your life. Keep learning.

Self-help books are another great learning tool. Many of the techniques that I use daily to enhance my life have been taught to me in self-help books. Reading them can give you valuable information that can't be found anywhere else. When put into action, the strategies mentioned in self-help books have the potential to greatly increase the quality of your life. Remember, confidence is built through progress, so any book you read that gives you tools to help you make progress in your life is a book worth reading.

To view some of my most highly recommended books, go to the following web address:

www.healthandhappinessfoundation.com/recommended-reading

Youtube Learning

I would estimate that 75% of everything I've learned about what it takes to become a confident and capable human being has been from Youtube videos. While others were watching music videos, standup comedy and all that, I was watching inspiring and motivational people show me how to be successful. It became kind of an addiction for me, but I'm glad to say it was an addiction that made me a better person. If you're like most people, you would probably rather watch a video than read a book, so why not make Youtube your primary learning tool? It has transformed my life, and I'm confident it can do the same for you.

Some of my favorite "Youtubers" are:

Elliott Hulse, Dan McDonald, Infinite Waters (Ralph Smart), Raw Brahs, Mooji, Brendon Burchard, and plenty more but that will get you started! You can also find my personal channel at BeauNorton.com

These Youtube channels have been responsible for a huge increase in my confidence. They have inspired me and led me to believe in myself and in the possibilities that life offers all of us. Sometimes it is hard to inspire and motivate ourselves, so it's never a bad idea to turn to others to do the job for us. There are countless people out there trying to lift people up and empower them. Don't be afraid to turn to these people for guidance. They just may change your life forever.

Emulate a Great

One of the fastest ways to become a confident person is to spend time with or study the life of someone who is already confident. Just as I mentioned earlier about emulating the body language of the people you want to be like, you can also emulate a person's thought processes and behaviors to become more like them. My suggestion to you is for you to find one person that you admire above all others and find out as much about that person as you possibly can. This can be a family member, professional athlete, celebrity, or whoever that has the character traits and lifestyle that you would like to have. Find out everything you can about this person. Read books about them, watch videos and interviews of them, and talk to them in person if possible. This person already has the qualities that you would like to possess, so by studying them you can view the actions that they took and the type of mindset that got them to where they're at. Now, all you have to do is cultivate a similar way of thinking and behaving, which can be done in part by using the thought restructuring exercises that I mentioned in the first chapter. The more you study the people you wish to be like, the more your thoughts and actions will become aligned with the type of life that they are living, and so it goes back to the "fake it 'til you make it" theory – act as if you're already there and soon you will be.

Addict Yourself to Success

Dedicate yourself to the study of what it takes to become a better human being. If you want to achieve your goals bad enough, you will make sacrifices to do so.

Perhaps you need to spend less time watching television or playing video games and more time developing yourself. I promise you it is more fun than it sounds. The time you spend on improving yourself will pay off a million fold in the long run. You must get over the mindset of instant gratification and quick fixes. You will struggle, and you will fail, but the satisfaction you get from watching yourself steadily improve over time cannot be explained in words. Make the choice today whether you are going to stay the same as you are or grow and evolve into a powerful, confident, happy, and successful person.

Chapter 5: Facing Fears

"Inaction breeds doubt and fear. Action breeds confidence and courage. If you want to conquer fear, do not sit home and think about it. Go out and get busy."

-Dale Carnegie

The greatest challenge will come on your journey to greater success and confidence when you are face to face with your biggest fear. When this time comes, you will have the option to stay where you are comfortable or to push forward through the resistance. If you fail to take action, you will never have the extreme confidence you desire. In fact, failure to take action when you know you need to will lower your confidence, so please take what you learn from this chapter and begin to use it immediately.

Facing your fears takes great courage. If you suffer from a lack of confidence, this task can seem near impossible. In this chapter, I will give you a step by step formula for building your courage so that you can face your fears more willingly and experience the increase in confidence that comes from doing so.

Small Steps Lead to BIG Change

If you jump right in and face your biggest fears before you take the time to develop your self-confidence, you risk falling flat on your face and destroying your self-esteem even further. By no means is failure a bad thing, but if you aren't prepared for it, it can do more harm than good. That is why it is important to start small and face your fears gradually. As you adapt to getting out of your comfort zone, tasks that would have previously been extremely intimidating become less of a challenge.

Make a list of things that scare you and rank them on a scale from 1 to 10 according to how difficult they would be for you to do. For example, walking up to a stranger and starting a conversation might be a 3 out of 10, and giving a speech in front of 1,000 people might be a 9 or 10. Keep adding to this list until you have at least 2 or 3 things for each level of difficulty. Once you complete the list, it is time to begin taking action. Start with the tasks that are a 1 out of 10 difficulty for you and continue to do them until they become relatively easy for you to do. Go at your own pace but continue to take action on a consistent basis, even if you have to stay on the lower difficulties for a long time. Move your way up the scale and your comfort zone will slowly expand. It may take a year or two for you to get to the 9's and 10's on your list, but the important thing is that you are growing and evolving into a better person during the process. You will soon find that you are capable of doing things you never would have thought possible before, and your confidence will increase as you get more and more experience with facing your fears.

It is important to know that facing your fears will never be a comfortable experience. You will always experience anticipatory anxiety when facing an unfamiliar situation, but building your courage will allow you to jump into these situations without thinking too much about it. Once you actually do the thing, the fear usually dissipates and the whole experience becomes quite rewarding. Do not expect to eliminate fear, because it will always be there. Do expect, however, to build your courage to a point where fear is no longer an obstacle.

Accountability Partners

It can be very difficult to face your fears if you don't have a compelling reason to do so. A study was once done that discovered people are twice as likely to avoid pain as they are to seek pleasure. So, personal growth and increased confidence may not be a compelling enough reason for you to willingly face your fears. Perhaps you should focus on what you *don't* want instead.

A great way to ensure that you take action is to create a situation where the consequences of not doing what you need to do are greater than the fear of doing it. You will need an accountability partner for this, which is just someone that can hold you to your word. So, for example, you tell your friend (accountability partner) that you will approach a beautiful woman and ask for her phone number, or else you have to give him or her 50 dollars. Give them the money to hold on to first, and tell them not to give it back unless you do what you said you would. Most people aren't willing to give up 50 bucks, so the fear of losing the money will be greater than the fear of approaching the woman. You can do this with just about anything you choose. If there is something you know you need to do, find an accountability partner that you can trust and tell them your plan. Using money for this works very well, because people do not like to lose money and often times would rather completely embarrass themselves than give it up. Remember, fear is the greatest motivator. Use it to your advantage!

Fear is a Blessing

Everyone experiences fear. It is a natural response to unfamiliar situations. With society evolving at such a rapid pace, unfamiliarity is very common. However, I believe that unfamiliarity and unpredictability is what makes life exciting. Excitement and fear are almost identical emotions, the only difference being the way we label those emotions. Next time you feel afraid, rethink the situation and consider that maybe you're just excited! At the least, know that everyone has fears and insecurities and that being afraid does not make you weak or any less capable of achieving greatness. In fact, fear is a blessing. When you overcome fears, you are generously rewarded with increased confidence and self-esteem. Without fear, you would never know how great it feels to overcome challenges and evolve into a stronger version of yourself. I promise you, the struggle is worth it. Carry on and stay strong, my friend.

Conclusion: Create a Cycle of Positivity

There was a time in my life when I felt as if everything around me was falling apart. My self-esteem was at an all-time low. I was absolutely miserable and I didn't know why, but soon I realized that I had simply gotten myself into a vicious downward spiral. I knew that if I didn't reverse the cycle, I would suffer for most of my life. So, I made the decision that I was going to do whatever it took to become happy and live the life of my dreams. I've been in an upward spiral ever since, and I'm only gaining more and more momentum as time goes by. I say this because my mission in life is to inspire others and let them know that no matter where they stand currently, major positive change is possible with the right knowledge. This book discusses many of the tools I used to drastically improve my life, and now I share them with you so that you may do the same. You deserve to live the life of your dreams. However, it is up to you to go make It happen.

It all starts with your mindset. In order to achieve your goals, you have to believe that it is possible. If you are just starting the journey of personal development, focus first on creating a positive attitude. This can be done by using the strategies in chapter one. Learn to love yourself fully. Don't place so much importance on the opinions of other people. You cannot build self-confidence when you are being bombarded with the negativity of the world. Separate yourself from that at all costs, even if it means moving to another state or ending a long standing relationship.

Surround yourself with positive people, emulate the greats, and face your fears head on. With every ounce of positivity you feed your mind, body, and spirit, you gain momentum in the direction of your dreams. Reaching your goals becomes increasingly easier, and your small successes build on one another to create something magnificent.

Extreme confidence is just a byproduct of success. With every small success, you will experience an increase in confidence. Set a compelling goal that gets you moving, and then focus on the journey. Whatever you do, just keep moving forward.

Thank you for taking the time to read this book. I hope that you apply these methods and experience greater success as a result. For more motivation for your personal transformation, visit my blog at

HealthandHappinessFoundation.com

ALPHA VS. VAMPIRE

VAMPIRE REC

— J

ELLIE SCOTT

Copyright © 2017

Ellie Scott

INTRODUCTION

The rival between wolves and vampires is a dance that has been going on since the dawn of time. Nevertheless, that did not stop Casper for falling for the one wolf that was off limits, Raygan's baby sister Kylee who had ascended to alpha after his death.

She was gorgeous, dangerous and had stolen his heart from the first time he had met her.

Aside from the fact that they should be born enemies, he was now faced with a dilemma- revenge. When Jack had killed her brother, he had started a war that could only be stopped by his death.

A life for a life. Kylee would have it no other way.

Caught in the middle was Jack's love, Maya. The vampires knew that there was something different about this pack of wolves. Their deadly venom was not much of a secret in the vampire world but what would it mean for one of their own? This was no longer the battle between species. It was a battle against time to save love before love killed them all.

3

Ellie Scott

TABLE OF CONTENTS

Ellie Scott

LEGAL NOTES

Ellie Scott

CHAPTER 1.

Maya looked out at the freshly washed forest. It had been raining almost non-stop for two weeks. It was as if the wolves who had been howling the loss of their leader at somehow caused the weather to mirror their pain. Well, that was if you thought of rain as sadness. Her grandmother had always told her to look at is as something simply washing away the dirt to expose the beauty beneath.

Standing here looking out at the lush foliage, she had to agree.

"Thinking of finally going out there?" Casper came up behind her.

She turned and glared at him. "How many times am I to tell you not to sneak up on me? You are going to give me a heart attack one day."

9

He looked almost hurt as he stared at her. "I didn't mean to. It's just that-"

"Yes. Yes. I know. Vampire and all that stealthy goodness. Just stop though."

She turned back to the window and he leaned against the wall looking at her. "You have been inside this house for two weeks. And don't get me wrong, it has been nice having you around, but don't you think you should get out for a bit."

She had been thinking the same thing. "But Jack said..."

"Where is Jack?" Casper asked him sounding annoyed.

That was a damn good question. She had not seen him for days and she didn't know if she was to assume he was dead, or maybe just that he had had enough of her for a while and needed a break.

"I don't know," she whispered.

"Exactly," Casper replied. "I will take you into town if you want me to."

She smiled and agreed. She couldn't understand why Jack would have wanted a break from her if that was his reason for disappearing. In the two weeks that she had been here they had talked, laughed and even kissed a few times, but he always kept his distance.

Alpha vs. Vampire

She didn't know if maybe he regretted having her here or was just afraid. He would watch her with such care in his eyes, and then when she got too close or he got too comfortable, he would just disappear for hours. It was a strange thing that had her checking if maybe she was the problem.

Yeah, she definitely needed to get out of here for a while.

Walking down the hall to the lush room he had made her own, she threw some of her things into a duffle bag, hauled on a jacket and headed for the door.

"Where are you two going?" Aiden asked. He was ever the watchful one. Apparently the eldest too. Why it was that Jack was seemingly the leader if age defined the hierarchy was something that had piqued her curiosity several times.

"I am going home for a while. If Jack comes back anytime soon, please let him know."

"Hmmm," Aiden said casting a wary glance around the woods. "Be careful."

How could she forget not to be? Jack had made it clear the wolves would come, and they would come when they all least expected it. She had made it her point of duty to always be expecting them.

11

"I will be," she promised him with a kiss to his cheek.

She smiled thinking how she had always been made to believe by myths and legends that vampires were to feel cold to the touch. These men were warm; nothing about them seemed dead. It was a comforting difference to the tales of time.

"Hop on!" Casper said, and she did just that.

Having been used to riding with Jack, she was not prepared for the speed Casper rode with. In record time, they hit the highway and minutes later they were parked outside her apartment.

It was quiet. Just way too quiet.

She looked up to see if Mike's head would poke out form his balcony like it usually did at the sound of any vehicle in the parking lot...nothing.

"It's too quiet here," she whispered to Casper, almost afraid to break the silence that was almost reverent.

He looked around them, but seemed to relax.

"It has been quiet since Raygan," he referenced the execution she had watched happen right in front of her.

Maya had spent a whole lot of time processing that too. It was one thing to see a street fight, a totally different one to see someone executed- arguably on her behalf. After all, the alpha had said he would kill her if he ever got the chance. More so, she had heard the vampires' side of the story, but not the wolves'. It would be interesting to see if they actually coincided or there would be disparity. Her grandmother had always said there were four sides to every story. In this case, it would be the wolves' side, the vampires', the truth and most importantly what she chose to believe.

It was highly unlikely that she would ever get the other side to this coin though. As far as the wolves were concerned, she was directly involved in Raygan's death, and they were not going to take that lightly.

"I will walk you up," Casper said.

She couldn't help thinking that Jack should have been here to do it, but such was life as she was beginning to understand it.

The walk in the stairwell was uneventful. Her apartment smelt like it hadn't been visited for a long time. When Casper had a look around and was sure everything was alright he told her that if she wanted to go out to call him.

"It's not safe for you," he reiterated. "I will be in the town. Call me if you need me."

"Thanks, but I will be okay."

He smiled. "You will be because I will be there."

"That's Jack's job. He isn't here so don't worry about it."

Casper must have sensed her anger rising and decided not to poke the bear.

"First sign of trouble, just call," he begged as he let himself out.

She sighed in relief. Until then she had not known how much she missed her own space and the lack of people in it. She needed to sleep, and after a long hot shower in a place that was familiar, she did just that.

Alpha vs. Vampire

Ellie Scott

CHAPTER 2.

Casper stayed in the tree line outside of Maya's apartment, circling to make sure she was okay. He had half expected her to come back out of the building like the rebellious teenager she could be, but she stayed put. He could understand why.

Just as the night took over the town, he stole up the staircase to check on her. He stood at the door and listened to the steady beating of her heart and the slow shallow breaths she took and knew she was fast asleep.

"Good girl," he muttered and dashed down the stars before anyone could see him. He had some place to be.

The rain started up a light drizzle as he ran through the forest heading towards the place he had missed

17

since all this death had taken over his life. He was intent on seeing the one person who had come to mean more to him than life.

Slowing as he approached the rundown old abandoned house in the woods, he quickly climbed a tree and took in the place. He didn't expect even the wolf pack to be this deep in the forest, but with Raygan's death and Jack constantly missing, anything was possible.

He listened and heard nothing but his faint breathing and the sound of blood rushing through his veins. He could not hear a single heartbeat within miles and sadness swept over him. Maybe he was just early. He wanted to believe that, but the position of the young moon in the sky told him he was actually a little late. Maybe, just maybe, this was how it would be going forward but he still waited.

Pretty soon it paid off, as a familiar shrouded figure appeared from the south of the building. Whoever it was stuck to the shadows avoiding where all the traps had been set as they entered the building. He smiled.

He hopped down and followed in their footsteps. The entrance to the building was covered in bushes and he was sure not to disturb them as he entered. The crumbling walls that formed the hallway smelt like muss and things ancient and old, but it did not bother him.

Alpha vs. Vampire

"Hi, my love," he whispered to the figure pacing ahead of him.

She lifted the cloak that hid her face and her fiery red eyes pulled him in. To many others, she was the thing to fear. To him, she was simply Kylee, the woman who stole his heart.

Or rather the wolf who stole his heart.

She didn't say a single thing, but the tears in her eyes shun bright. He rushed to her side and pulled her against him.

"I am sorry," he whispered in her white hair. "I am so sorry."

She sobbed uncontrollably in his arms and he held her. He held her because the pain that brought those tears to her eyes was a pain he knew all too well. The loss of the people you loved.

"Why did you let him kill my brother?" she asked him, the red fading from her eyes to be replaced by amber that echoed the pain in her heart.

"I am sorry my love, but Raygan is the only person responsible for his own death. We tried to talk to him and he wouldn't listen. He promised that if Jack didn't kill him then and there he would go after everybody we loved."

19

"Including the human," Kylee said sounding angry. For a moment, the flash of red ignited again, but then it died just as quickly. It was hard to be angry when you were hurting. According the five steps of grief, the anger would come soon enough, and Casper knew all too well there would be hell to pay.

"Her name is Maya," Casper whispered, wiping her tears away. "And she really didn't deserve to die because we couldn't get the people we love to get along."

"My brother must be avenged," she said to him, stepping away.

Casper sighed. "I only ask that you take time to mull this over Kylee. In all the years since this pointless war has started, when did revenge ever turn out well for any of us? I don't want you to make the same mistakes your brother did. If anything were to happen to you I would not survive."

"I am alpha now," she said turning to him. "If I leave things as is, it will be a sign to my pack that I am either too afraid of the vampires or I didn't care about my brother. Neither assumption will do us any good. And when it comes out that I am in love with you, they will try to kill you to exact revenge. I am alpha Casper. It is not just about you and me anymore."

He sighed yet again. "You are alpha now, and this is a chance for you to choose to lead differently. Don't turn away from the old ways, but build more positively on them. None of us want to see more bloodshed because egos were bruised."

She stepped up to him and ran her thumb across his cheeks before pressing a soft kiss to his lips.

"This is not about egos, my love," she said walking away. "Just remember that no matter what happens, I have always loved you and I always will."

She walked away without so much as another word and he was left with a decision. Maybe it was time to come clean to Jack and the others. They needed to know that the threat was not just as simple as vampires against wolves in an age-old cliché of attacks. This time they would be fighting a pack led by someone with more cunning and strength than Raygan could have ever dreamt of in his lifetime. The only reason he had ascended to alpha before Kylee was because he was older by a couple years. What the pack had that made them unique came from her existence.

And her venom was more lethal than any of them could even imagine.

Ellie Scott

CHAPTER 3.

It was the soft brush of cold fingers against her temple that jolted her awake this time. When she slid to the edge of the bed, she was looking at a face she wanted to kiss and smash in at the same time.

"Where have you been?" she asked him angrily.

Jack looked as if he was trying to find an excuse but had none.

"I cooked you dinner," he chose to say instead and it was only then that she recognized the smell of pot roast and something else coming from her kitchen.

"You don't cook," she said accusingly, rudely shoving him out of the way and heading to the living room where food was laid out on her table as if he expected a starving army to pass through.

"I cook," he admitted with a smile. "And I am bloody good at it."

"I wouldn't know" she muttered taking a piece of meat from the pile. Her stomach groaned in anticipated gratitude and she remembered she hadn't eaten in hours.

"That is no way to treat your boyfriend," he feigned disappointment.

"Boyfriend?" she asked with a chuckle. "So, we are dating now? How cute."

He poured her a glass of wine from the bottle on the table and handed it to her. "We aren't dating?"

He sounded almost confused, but she was not falling for it.

"No, we are not. Dating involves…dates!" she glared at him. "It involves you being present to smooch on me, romance me and feeling me up. You aren't feeling me up! Nobody is feeling me up! I got felt up more when I was single and working in a dive bar than I do now that I am supposed to be dating you! So, mister, I am very single."

"I can change that," he said taking the glass from her and pushing her up against the wall. For a moment,

Alpha vs. Vampire

Maya lost herself in the sweetness of his kiss before she remembered she was angry at him.

"No! You are not getting off the hook so easily."

She shoved him away and sat at the table. She piled an enormous amount of food on her plate with no idea how she was going to eat it all.

"I guess I should feed you more often," he joked as she stuffed her mouth.

"Yeah, a boyfriend who isn't even around to feed me after he locked me away in a mausoleum with other dead people walking about."

"Aiden will take great offense to that," he sipped his wine and stared at her. "You are cute when you are upset."

She chomped angrily at her food and tossed a broccoli at him. "You are insufferable! Where have you been?"

He sat across from her and popped the broccoli into his mouth. "Making sure it was safe for you to come out of the house when you decided to."

"No..." she muttered. "Please don't tell me you killed others.

He stared at her in disappointment. "I am not a killer Maya. I would never willingly take another life even if it was the life of my enemy. I only did what I had to do to protect you."

"I know," she sighed. "I am sorry."

"I spent days trying to talk to the wolves, but their new alpha wouldn't even show up."

"New alpha?" she asked him.

"Yeah, word is that Raygan had a baby brother. He will naturally ascend to be their alpha, but I have never seen him. For now, the wolves seem docile and caught up with the change in management, but I know they will come and they will come for you first."

She sighed. "Lovely."

"I will be here though. They will have to pluck my heart from my chest to get to you."

She smiled at his words, knowing every single one of them were true.

Alpha vs. Vampire

Ellie Scott

CHAPTER 4.

Jack stayed with her for hours. The conversation that spun on mostly centered around what life would be like, arguing about her going back to work and him deciding she would not be working in that bar anymore.

"You can't just tell me I won't work in the bar. How do you think I will pay my bills?" she asked him a little frustrated that this part of the conversation was taking them nowhere.

"You could move back in with me and the guys," he said kissing her forehead.

She glared at him. "And become one of those women who live off the men they date? No, Sir-ee! The fact that you even suggested that means you don't even he admitted. "And every time I think I am getting close you do something else that surprises me and proves me wrong."

"That means you should spend more time getting to know me and less trying to dictate what I will do. If bossing me around is you aim, you won't get very far."

She walked away from him mostly because she needed a minute without his hands touching her. The truth was every time he walked into a room she had to remind herself not to be a groupie. This discussion they were having was so much more than a talk about the state of their union, or whatever the hell this was. It was a decision about her life going forward.

Why was this even a topic of importance?

The simple reason is because out of all the men she could have fallen for in this bloody town, she had to fall for a vampire who didn't understand boundaries and came with a slew of venomous wolf-like enemies, who wanted to have her for dinner, breakfast and lunch. Though this seemed to be par for the course for her love life; she never could get it right. She should have gone for a recluse who didn't go anywhere long enough for people to have vendettas against him. Come to think of it, she might just become a recluse herself.

Alpha vs. Vampire

"Tell me Maya," he whispered across the room to her. It was a seductive pull she had learnt to ignore.

"Tell you what now?" she asked. "What should I tell you this time that you are simply going to ignore?"

He chuckled. "If you could own your own business, what would it be?"

She turned and looked at him in confusion.

"Tell me," he demanded with a smile.

"A book store," she said shyly and looked away. "I would own a book store that dealt in rare books as well as just about anything readable, with a small room for reading and a cafe out front for those who simply wanted to stop by for coffee."

"Sounds nice," he said.

She turned to him suddenly. "Don't mock me. I love books and I was actually saving towards that dream. My grandmother and I used to talk about it all the time."

"I am not mocking your dream, my love," he came to stand behind her as she stared out at the night below them. "I actually think it sounds lovely."

She smiled and leaned back into his embrace. "More than anything else I dreamt of that."

"Okay, let's make it happen," he said kissing the top of her head.

She turned to look up at him. "Don't play jokes like that!"

Cupping her face, he kissed her forehead. "I am not. Tomorrow we will find you a shop space and we will get the help you need for design, procuring books and all those other things that come with the store. You will have your store."

"I don't have the money," she said.

"I do, and lots of it. Why not spend it on the dreams of the woman I love?"

She smiled up at him. "So, you love me, huh?"

His face took on a seriousness she had never seen before. It was as if a whole new emotion had swept through him, but she did not feel as if she was in danger. She felt safe.

"I love you Maya," he whispered. "Don't ever forget that. I would give my life if it meant you would be safe. I would give my life if it meant you would have everything you dreamt of."

Alpha vs. Vampire

She had no words. Not because she didn't love him too, but because she was so afraid to admit that out loud right now. Looking into his eyes she saw that he too knew that. And so, they went to bed with fingers interlocked and her head over his chest.

"Tomorrow we go to town early and get started on making your dreams come true," he said as she drifted off to sleep.

The smell of breakfast woke her that morning and she ventured into the kitchen to see him bare chest making her eggs and bacon.

"Morning love," he smiled and placed a plate before her.

"You really do cook," she laughed.

"Only for you," he replied. "Now eat up we have a long day ahead of us."

That was the truth. By noon they had found her the perfect shop with a patio for the cafe. Casper, Aiden and even Cassian came by to help, threatening the men who tried to tax her too heavily for the task she was about to carry out. Outside of prying eyes, and with the windows covered with newspaper they moved with lightning speed and a frightening amount of strength to get the inside of the book store the way she wanted it. By late evening the space was resembling the beginnings of her vision and a contractor was on call to have the cafe up and running in three days.

She was excited and tired beyond words.

"I have a gift for you," Jack said later that evening after she had showered and he had made her a meal once again.

She looked around for this mysterious gift but saw nothing in sight. "What is it?"

"You can have a collection of my rare books for your bookstore. As long as you promise me they won't be sold."

She squealed and jumped into his arms. "I wanted to ask you, but I wasn't so sure you would say yes. In the reading room, I want to have books that can be read there. Those would be nice."

"Good," he said. "Now go to sleep. Tomorrow you can pick them out."

He took his jacket up as he spoke.

"Where are you going?" she asked him.

He looked away shyly. "I must feed my love. You worked me to the bone today."

"Oh," she said and looked away. "I completely forgot about that part of things."

He kissed her and was gone in the single breath of that moment. She missed him already. Deciding to go do her laundry she hauled her basket down the stairs, only coming back when she was through.

"So, this is who all the fuss is about?" she heard a sultry female voice say from the shadows of her bedroom.

Maya instantly turned to bolt for the door, but a strong arm held her back.

"Where are you going?" a deep voice asked. The light switch came on and she was looking into a very familiar face.

"Mike?" she questioned. "What are you doing?"

"I warned you to stay away from them," he said. Now she understood why he had spoken so vehemently against her connection with Jack, despite there not being any at the time.

The woman chuckled behind her. "And we all know that the ones who cannot hear are the ones who must feel."

Ellie Scott

Maya's breath left her as she looked at the most beautiful woman she had ever seen. A flawless chocolate face with long flowing white hair, a body to die for and her eyes... they were changing so rapidly she couldn't keep track of their color.

"Who are you and what do you want?" Maya asked her. She was trying hard to not sound like some fragile little girl, but that wasn't working so well for her at the moment.

"I am Kylee," the woman said coming to stand before her, her eyes now a bloody red. "And for the murder of my brother I want revenge."

Maya watched as fangs extended form Kylee's mouth and they dripped a green liquid that sizzled as it touched the floor. Then she knew instantly. The way Mike looked at this woman and the fact that the only murder she was aware of was Raygan's, she knew Jack had it wrong.

Raygan didn't have a baby brother; he had left behind a sister. And hell hath no fury like a woman's wrath. If she didn't warn him somehow, he would never see the enemy coming. However, Kylee had other plans.

She grabbed Maya's hand and bit into it. The pain she felt was excruciating beyond words. When Mike let her go she crumbled to the floor and curled up in pain.

Alpha vs. Vampire

"Do stay alive long enough to deliver a message for me," Kylee said, stooping to look at her.

"Tell your boyfriend I will kill all the people he loves one by one unless he rights the wrong he did. And if he finds you in time, tell him I can heal you, but it comes with a price."

She laughed as she pulled her cloak over her head and went through the door. The last image she had was of Mike shaking his head at her as he made his exit. She looked at her phone a few meters away, but knew unless she had a guardian angel, she would not make it that far.

Her last thought as the pain took over, was that Jack would die if she didn't warn him.

Ellie Scott

CHAPTER 5.

Casper stared in shock at Kylee leaving Maya's apartment complex. He would have run up to her and demanded to know what the hell she was doing, but he couldn't risk that. He couldn't risk that with the three wolves by her side. They weren't just regular wolves, these had some form of tribal markings across their faces and he had never seen them before. Even with all the superhuman strength he had, he knew he would have a hard time with them, so he stuck to the shadows and waited.

"Go ahead of me," she ordered her men, looking around in the shadows.

He knew she couldn't see him, but being as powerful as she was, he knew it was not hard for her to pick him out of the darkness he wore like a second skin.

Ellie Scott

"We can't leave you here," one of the men replied, narrowing his eyes at her.

He watched as Kylee stepped up to him and stared him dead in the eyes.

"Let me be clear. I am not my brother and I am in no mood to explain myself or argue a point. I said leave me and that is what I meant."

Even amidst all the chaos he was sure would soon ensue, he had to smile. She was a badass!

"I know you are here Cass," she called out when the men were far enough away that he could not hear their heartbeats or footsteps.

He stepped out of the shadows so she could see him and then turned and headed into the tress. Her light footsteps followed him.

"What are you doing here?" he asked her immediately.

"Are you following me?" she asked and he could see anger flash in her eyes for a moment.

"Would you blame me if I were?"

She glared at him. "Yes!"

Alpha vs. Vampire

Casper really didn't want an argument. "I showed up in time to see you leaving... I came to check on Maya, but seems you beat me to it."

"You know what will be the death of you vampires? Your love for humans."

For a moment, Casper did not recognize the woman whose soulful eyes had stolen his heart. He had remembered her talking years ago about how happy she was that her brother had the burden of alpha to bare. She had relished that fact because it was a position that came with the need to make decisions that were inhumane more often than not. Yet, here she was wearing her face but with his attitude. He had no idea how to respond to that.

"Kylee, listen to me," he said resting his hands on her shoulders. "You cannot let vengeance and power change you. I know the pain of losing the only family you have left. I know it more than you could ever understand, but your actions today decide how long you will have to fight and how many more you will have to lose."

"Well, tell Jack he holds the key to the peace you so fervently seek. His life in exchange for Maya's."

"What?" Casper asked confused. "What are you talking about?"

41

Ellie Scott

"I will have blood for blood Cass," she said looking at him so he could not miss her point. "I must avenge my brother. And Maya will die in a day if Jack is still alive. The only person who can stop the venom making its way to her heart is me, and I will not do that unless Jack gives me his life. A life for a life."

Casper let her go and looked towards Maya's apartment. "What have you done Kylee?"

"A life for a life," she repeated as he stepped away from her and dash up the stairs to Maya's apartment.

The door was unlocked and if he had a heartbeat it would have stopped just then and there. Covered in black veins from head to toe, Maya laid writhing in pain.

"No! No! No! No!" he shouted as he ran to her side.

"Casper," she managed to croak out as she choked on the blood draining from her mouth. "Help me..."

Her words trailed off as she started to shake uncontrollably. He was at a loss as to what could be done, but he knew no human hospital could cure what was wrong with her. Cassian maybe could. Without another thought he lifted her into his arms and headed straight for the forest. As he passed the tree-line he saw Kylee smile and turned back into the night. He didn't recognize her. There was nothing of the woman he loved there.

He had more pressing issues now though. If Maya died, nothing would stop Jack for declaring war and they had all already lost too much.

At lightning speed, he dashed through the forest towards the mansion. He could hear footsteps following him just as quickly as he went and could smell Aiden as he approached. He must have been on guard somewhere close by.

"What is wrong with her?" Aiden asked, matching his pace.

"Wolf bite," he replied as he hopped over a tree trunk and burst onto the well-manicured lawn.

"Shit" was the only thing Aiden could say as he flung the door open for him.

Casper gave no further explanation, but he knew he would have to soon. The bite was no regular wolf venom. This would not be one their vampire blood could easily heal. When they had first been informed the wolves had evolved somehow, it had been ages ago. A human had died and a vampire had been so sick he shrunk to skin and bones before they figured out that vampire blood on the wound could ease the effects until a mixture of vervain and wolf blood had been consumed as the cure. It was no easy mixture to

Ellie Scott

drink and even the strongest of vampires would have to bare the effects of the burn vervain gave once consumed if they wanted to survive.

Over the years Cassian had tried his best to trace the origins of the wolves' new abilities, but he hadn't gotten any further than to find that Raygan's father did not have the ability nor the wolves before him. It somehow started with Raygan and seemingly evolved with Kylee. It was a mystery he had never asked her about, because divulging the secret could put her pack in harm's way and he would never put her in that position.

He was thinking now he might have to.

"What the hell is this?!" Cassian shouted as they rested Maya carefully on her bed and stood back. The black veins now covered her entire body, and though she was breathing calmly she seemed to have fallen into a deep sleep.

"Maya…" Cassian called softly. There was no reply.

"Is she dead?" Aiden asked.

Casper glared at him. "No stupid! She's still breathing."

"Hmmm," Aiden replied unperturbed by Casper's name calling.

"Maybe death would be a more convenient welcomed relief for whatever is in her system," Cassian replied and Casper had to agree.

He knew he would have a lot more explaining to do and as Jack burst into the room he knew his moment of reckoning had come.

"No! Maya," he wailed as he pulled her into his arms. The only indication that she was still alive was the fact that she was breathing. Her limp body gave no other indication that she was still with them.

"How could you let this happen?" Jack asked him kissing her forehead and glaring at him. "Where were you?!"

"I got there after it happened," he said calmly. "There is something I need to tell you all.

But first, we have to try the vervain," Casper said as he stepped out of the room coming back moments later with a syringe and a vervain and blood mix.

Casper knew it probably might not work, because no regular wolf had bitten her, but they had to try. Maybe it would spare him the torrent of shit storm that was about to come his way. He stood to the side and watched Cassian work. It wasn't long before the black veins faded and Maya's eyes opened.

45

They were the feral red he had come to know very well. The feral red of Kylee's when she was upset.

"What the hell kind of wolf bit her?" Aiden asked staring at her in shock.

"Raygan's sister," Maya whispered. It was barely audible and Casper closed his eyes and shook his head in despair.

Shit!

"Did she just say Raygan's sister?" Aiden asked.

Jack looked at her confused. "Yes, but it must be the poison."

"No!" Maya tried to shout. "Listen to me Jack. The new alpha is not a man. It's a woman and she says she will have your life for the life of her brother, and the only way to save me is with her blood. She won't give it until you give her your own."

Silence fell around the room and Casper could see they were all grappling with whether to believe Maya's struggling breath and the seeming impossibility of her words.

Casper decided not to wait any longer. "It's true."

All eyes turned to him as Maya drifted off to sleep in Jack's arms.

"What do you mean?" Cassian asked him.

With a sigh, he spoke. "Years ago, I met and fell in love with a woman."

"We know," the men all said in unison.

"You know?!" he asked in shock.

"Yes, you kept sneaking off and you had a glow. Only a woman does that so we followed you one night when we were across the border in the south and we saw you. We decided to leave you be because maybe keeping her a secret was the only way to ensure she didn't get caught up in all this," Aiden said.

"But what does that have to do with Maya?" Jack asked.

"Her name is Kylee and she is Raygan's sister," he said.

The silence that ensued was no longer one of shock. He could see the mixture of emotions floating around the room. Mixed in was a trace of betrayal.

"What?!" Jack asked resting Maya on the bed and coming to stand in front of him.

"Before you pick a fight with me hear me out," Casper urged him. "When I met Kylee, she was trying to get

47

away from her pack. She wanted nothing to do with the wars Raygan raged everywhere he went, but we all know the bond of a wolf pack flows deeper than just geography. No matter where she went they always found her. She stayed close to me over the years that we travelled, occasionally running off for days with her pack and coming back. She was of no harm to us and barely knowledgeable of the power she had. Most of all, she was so happy Raygan was there to be alpha. Leading a pack was never something she wanted. She hated the very idea."

"Until I killed her brother and she ascended," Jack said.

"Yes."

"Shit!" Aiden muttered "But this is no regular wolf bite."

"No..." he conceded. "It is not, and that mix that Cassian gave her will only work for a short period before the poison takes over and eventually kill her. As far as I know, the only cure is Kylee's blood."

"Then go get some!" Jack demanded.

"She won't give it that easily. She wants your life, Jack, and she is no average wolf. She could take us all without the need for help. She is small but she is powerful. The kind of powerful that none of us can hope to defeat alone, and even with the four of us, taking her is going to be a task. Added to that, she is sorely upset that you killed her brother."

"He had to be stopped."

"I agree," Casper sighed. "And she does too, but he must be avenged."

"So, to save the woman I love, I have to give your psycho girlfriend my life?" Jack asked.

"She isn't crazy, she is an alpha. That fact comes with responsibilities and decisions none of us want to ever have to make. That is why she ran."

"Will she stand to reason?" Cassian the diplomat spoke up.

"I don't know, but we can try," Casper said. "I saw her earlier today after she had bitten Maya. I didn't recognize her Cass. I didn't see Kylee in those eyes. I didn't see the woman I loved anywhere."

Jack pulled him in for a hug. "We will figure it out, and if sacrificing my life saves the women we love then I am ready and willing to do just that."

"I can't let you do that," Casper whispered to the man who had become his brother and best friend.

"We might not have a choice," he said. "Take me to her. We are taking Maya, because I don't know how much longer she has and I cannot live with the thought of her death."

Aiden sighed. "The one thing I know for sure is that neither Kylee nor Maya deserved anything our existence gave them to deal with."

"And that is a wrong we have to right."

Casper sighed again. Morals will be the death of them one day. If only Raygan had been like that, then they wouldn't be here today.

Alpha vs. Vampire

Ellie Scott

CHAPTER 6.

Casper watched as they wrapped a sleeping Maya as warmly as they could and with the darkness as their guide he led them through the forest and into town to the mansion on the other side that served as a compound for the wolves. He wasn't sure what was about to happen here, but he knew that it would change their lives yet again.

He probably shouldn't be so worried about change. After all, it was the only thing that was constant in life. His greatest fear was that he would lose the woman he loved. Jack never backed down without a fight.

"How much further?" Cassian asked.

He didn't need to answer. The men sitting on the perimeter of the wall looking out at the night was as much of an answer that they needed. They would

53

have looked like normal men to the average eyes, but they were anything but.

"Get Kylee!" one man shouted. A young boy no more than fifteen ran off to do his bidding and the other men formed a guard at the wall.

"We are here," Casper announced the obvious.

Jack stepped forward. "We don't want a fight here in the streets. Your leader sent us an invitation. We are here to accept."

"Your death is the only accepted currency here," one man said.

Jack sighed. "Then so be it. However, I don't think you have the power to do that, so take me to her and stop wasting my time."

That wasn't a comment that was well received but it had the desired effect. They were led up a set of cobblestoned staircases to a well-lit foyer, beyond which they could see an open courtyard, large pool, tables for lounging and more wolves than they had ever seen in any one place. Over their heads the large house rose up three stories, and from what they could see, no expenses were spared in outfitting it. It was gorgeous by all definitions.

"The wolves aren't short on cash or style," Aiden whispered.

Alpha vs. Vampire

"What did you think?" Kylee's voice said from behind them. "Did you think we would be holed up in some den someplace in the woods, feeding off every carcass that floated by?"

They didn't answer and she smiled.

"No, that is just something you vampires do. We have more class than that."

"Your girlfriend is a tad bit of a bitch," Aiden whispered to him.

"Shhh," Casper urged him.

Kylee laughed as she came to stand before them. There was nothing warm about her laugh. It was sinister and almost pure evil.

"No, let him talk babe," she said to him. "More reason to feed you all to the angry wolves surrounding you."

And she was not joking. When he took his eyes off her for a moment he could see that where there had been twenty wolves, now stood an army larger than he could count. This was not going to be an easy fight to get out of.

"Kylee, we can talk about this. None of us wants any more bloodshed and no more lives to be lost."

She turned to him and what he saw in her eyes as they flashed blue was nothing but heartache and despair. He wanted to pull her into him and promise that it would all be okay. He would have, but her anger resurfaced and the hope of that was lost.

"Cure her," Jack demanded.

"For that, you will have to first give me your life," Kylee turned her attention to him. Casper knew then and there that it was no longer in his hands.

"It is yours once I know she is okay."

Kylee pointed to a table to the left. "Rest her down there."

Jack did as she asked. The young wolf who had sounded their arrival stepped forward with a syringe and a vial of blood. Kylee prepared the injection.

"How do I know that what you are giving her won't kill her?" Jack grabbed her hand and a group of wolves surged forward.

"Relax!" she ordered them. Her white hair flashing around her face as she turned to them. "I am not my brother, Jack. If I give my word you can count on it. This is my blood and she won't last much longer without it. You can either stand there and argue with me while she dies or we can get this over with."

Alpha vs. Vampire

He let her arm go and Casper breathed a sigh of relief. Kylee looked at him before she turned her attention back to where Maya laid on the table as if asleep. It was as if she was trying to tell him something in those fleeting glances, but he couldn't quite figure out what it was.

When Kylee withdrew the needle from Maya's hand, the black veins immediately receded, but her eyes did not open to put them all at ease.

"It will take a while," Kylee said. "She is human. Why you vampires are always obsessed with human girls when they are so fragile is something I will never understand."

"Maybe because they have souls and hearts," Aiden said.

Kylee laughed. "And you think we do not?"

No response was given except the movement from two of her guards towards Jack. They all moved to protect him and the response from the wolves was something reminiscent of war cries.

"No!" Jack said to them. "I gave my word. Just make sure Maya is safe."

"Kylee," Casper called. "Don't do this. We do not have to go about life the same way those before us did. All it ever did was cost lives and we should never be okay with that. Let us lead with a different kind of thinking."

She gazed at him lovingly and the blue in her eyes was unmistakable.

"I have loved you for as long as I can remember loving anyone," she said. "That fact alone was a betrayal to my pack, but they have swallowed it with a grain of salt because I was never meant to lead. I will always love you Casper, but I cannot teach my pack that it is okay for a vampire to kill one of our own and we do nothing. You and I have spoken about this before. Why are we here again?"

"Because this would mean war," he said simply and the pack shifted nervously around them. "Raygan came after Maya with no other intention but to hurt the vampires who wanted nothing but peace to begin with. Thirty years ago, he blew into town and destroyed all we had built. In the process, we lost everything and everyone. We left in defeat and now we are back, not to claim a city but to live in it as is our right. We were born and raised here, the wolves were not. We came back and made it clear we meant no harm. He came after us and Maya. Did you expect us to just let her die because your brother is a brat?"

"Was a brat," Kylee corrected him. "And it was never your right to take his life, so Jack must pay."

Alpha vs. Vampire

Her final words were an affirmation and beside him Jack was kicked to his knees by her guards. His hands were bent at the elbow and held up so his back was low and his head bent forward. From the coat that flowed around her trim body, Kylee pulled a Katana sword Casper had bought her as part of her collection years ago.

"Say your goodbyes," she urged Jack as she stood over him with the blade raised.

"Don't do this Kylee," he begged again as the wolves stepped in to surround each of them. His pleas fell on deaf ears, and he knew by the time he could fight his way over to her, Jack would already be dead.

Ellie Scott

CHAPTER 7.

Maya felt the cold table beneath her back and she could hear everything going on around her. She had been hearing everything since the bite but somehow, she could not move a muscle. It was like she was stuck in an incubator inside her own body. She had all her senses, but her eyes could not open and her mental screams fell on ears that could not hear her. She had felt Jack's arm around her and even more she could feel every single one of his emotions.

Am I dead? She thought. No, couldn't be. For she had felt the warmth of his hands leave her.

The table she laid on was cold and whatever she had been injected with was working. She had felt the warmth creeping slowly back into her body, but there was something else. As she listened to Kylee promise death to the vampire who had stolen her heart, she wrestled with this thing inside her. It was a force so strong she could barely control it.

"Say your last words," she heard Kylee urge again and in that moment her eyes shot open. She could see, but it was not the same. Her limbs seemed to move of their own volition as she sprung off the table honing in on where Jack was held for execution. Wolves moved towards her but they were no match for the strength she seemed to have been revived with. In a matter of seconds, she stood before Kylee with a rage unlike any she had ever felt before.

"Get away from him or I will kill every single one of you here."

A gasp went out in the crowd and Kylee's arm fell as the white-haired woman stared at her in shock. Maya looked at her confused, but even then, the wolves backed away.

"It cannot be," whispered Kylee.

Casper came to her side instantly. "Maya?"

"Your girlfriend is crazy," she said to him.

Casper stared at her in shock. "An argument can honestly be made for psychotic, but that is not the issue at hand here."

Alpha vs. Vampire

She had no idea what he was talking about and decided that focusing on Jack was more important. That was until he stood and looked at her strangely too. She sought refuge in Cassian's eyes, but the expressions he and Aiden wore were no different.

"Okay you crazy people, why are you all staring at me?"

The young wolf who had been by Kylee's side handed her a small mirror, and she nearly asked him how he conveniently had such a thing at a moment like this. She stopped short when she came full circle with the fact that nothing happened as it should these days. Anything was possible.

When she saw her reflection in the mirror, she understood how true that was.

Staring back at her were eyes as red and dangerous as that of any demon. Her face, once a mellow shade of caramel, was now black as the night outside the courtyard. Her ears were that of the wolves she had seen transformed and she had fangs.

She had fangs!

She looked down at her body and saw nothing else had changed, except her entire skin was black and her nails had turned into claws. She looked like a Halloween costume only she was very real.

"What the hell?!" she asked.

Kylee was the first to speak. "It is said that mutations are a source of impossibilities, and that is why I exist as I am."

She sheathed her sword and the wolves relaxed around her but still kept their distance.

"What are you talking about?" Maya asked her.

"Look," Kylee urged her and in the mirror her skin slowly changed back to its natural glow and so did every other feature that had changed.

"What the hell?!"

"A hybrid," Cassian spoke. "Before you there had only been talk of one other and that was before my time."

Kylee lifted the sword again and before she could stop herself, Maya grabbed it by the blade taking it from Kylee's hand and gripped the woman by the throat. Kylee fought back, but she was no match for Maya's strength.

"Behave or I will rip you to shreds," she warned.

"Let her go Maya," Casper said, resting his hand on her arm.

Alpha vs. Vampire

"If she promises to behave."

Kylee managed to nod and stepped away from her. The wolves followed.

"You just changed the nature of the game Maya," Cassian said.

"I don't know what that means but I would like to get out of here now."

Kylee stepped up to her again. "I got bitten by a black snake decades ago. When I changed the next time after that my fangs were filled with venom. I didn't tell anyone. When my father died and Raygan ascended to alpha, on the first full moon when we hunted as a pack, we discovered that all the wolves had venom. It was something we could not explain. For years, we tried to understand it, and thirty years ago we found an old Sage on the border of Canada who explained that wolves that have any kind of mutation in their blood can sometimes adapt to the dangers they are faced with. In my case, I got bitten by a lousy snake and instead of killing me, the venom somehow became a part of who I am. And because I come from a line of alpha's and was next in line to lead the pack, they would also share my abilities once we changed together on a full moon. Every wolf that has joined us since, once accepted, on the next full moon when they changed they get the same gift."

"Your point being," Maya asked.

Kylee chuckled. "My point being inexplicable things sometimes happen and the root explanation is really just our DNA."

"So, you are saying I have a mutation?"

"Yes," Cassian answered. "But never before have I experienced it like this. I gave you vervain mixed with vampire and wolf blood earlier. She gave you her own blood just now. You have the fangs of a wolf but the speed and look of an aged vampire. I assume your physical attribute somehow meshed the two."

"I don't hear her heart beating anymore," Jack said, tucking a strand of hair behind her ears.

It was then Maya realized she could no longer feel her heart beating. She hadn't even known before then that she somehow knew the sound of what gave her life. She panicked.

"She must have died at some point with the vampire blood you gave her Cass," Aiden said.

"Interesting," Kylee said looking at her.

Alpha vs. Vampire

The wolves seemed as intrigued and yet still afraid of her. They kept their distance and she started to feel like someone's science project.

"And she is strong. She could have just ripped Kylee to shreds," Casper said as if barely managing the reality that he could have just lost his love.

"Hybrids have one advantage over both wolves and vampires,' Cassian said smiling at her. "You are stronger than both species will ever be. And your existence just changed the rules of the game. We all know it."

"Her existence makes her a target," Jack groaned.

"My existence just saved your life and I would like to get out of here before they get any more ideas," she said looking at the wolves that stood uneasy around her.

"They won't harm you," Kylee said. "You can go."

"Just like that? You won't try to bite me again or anything."

"You could probably kill her before she even got close enough," Aiden laughed.

Maya didn't think it was funny. "Listen Kylee, killing people is never the answer to any problem you have and I know you don't want to admit this, but Raygan deserved what came to him. He was a liability for your pack. He would have killed and killed and more of your wolves would have died as those he hurt came after you for retaliation. Don't make the same mistakes your brother made. And I don't know what I am just yet but I know if you come after Jack I will kill you, and then I will have to deal with Casper and he is nice. He is a friend I don't want to ever have to hurt."

Kylee stood still listening to her speak, and when she looked at Casper her face softened.

"Teach your pack what it means to love and show them that vampires aren't so bad and we really don't need to be killing each other. No more death Kylee. Just no more."

She didn't give a response and they didn't wait for one. Jack took her hand and they walked slowly back the way he had carried her.

"Do you think they bought it?" Aiden asked.

It was Cassian who answered. "They will come for her, but not now. Now they know that she could mean all their deaths, so for now and maybe even a couple more decades Maya managed to grant us the peace we want."

"At what cost?" Jack said as they walked into the trees with the wolf pack staring after them.

Alpha vs. Vampire

"My life," she answered. "If I have no heartbeat it means I lost my life for this."

A pensive silence followed them back to the mansion where she sank into bed after a hot shower.

"What will happen to me now?" she asked Jack as he pulled her into his arms.

"For now, you will sleep. Tomorrow Cassian will want to poke and prod you and the rest we will take a day at a time."

"And the wolves?"

"For now, you don't have to worry about them."

She knew the truth to his words as he spoke them. "Don't ever do that to me again."

"Do what?" he asked.

"Try to die."

Jack kissed her lips softly. "To save your life I will always be willing to give my own. I love you and that is what love is."

She knew there was no arguing with him and so she said the only thing she really wanted to.

"I love you too, Jack."

69

Ellie Scott

CHAPTER 8.

Casper waited until they were all settled in before he looked for Cassian.

"You want to go see your girl?" Cassian asked from the shadows.

"Yes, do you think that is wise?"

"If it were Maya out there being all crazy, I would risk it all to have her back in my arms," Jack said joining the conversation.

"Think she will want to see me?"

Jack squeezed his shoulder. "If she loves you as much as she says she does then yes. Pack or not she will want to see you. Go and tell her I understand why she wanted to do what she did, I harbor no grudges."

Ellie Scott

Casper looked at them and smiled. He dashed out into the night moments later, making his way to where he had secretly met with Kylee since coming back to town. He could hear the slow beating of her heart before he stepped inside the ruin.

"I didn't think you would come," she said to him as she rushed into his arms.

"I will always come back to you," he whispered in her hair.

They stood in a sweet embrace filled with a promise of forever.

"No more bloodshed," she whispered in his chest. "I would have killed Jack because it was my duty to, but I hope you know I never wanted to."

"Is this because what Maya has become is a threat to you all, Kylee? Or is this the you I fell in love with coming back to me?"

"I have changed," she told him. "My responsibilities have changed me, but I will always be me and the things I valued before will never change. Including my love for you."

"Will your pack accept me being with you?" he asked.

"Ask them yourself," she replied and it was then he could hear the sounds of footsteps outside.

Alpha vs. Vampire

When he stepped out, the wolves stood in the clearing with the rising sun to their backs. Casper's fight or flight response took hold of him, but they kept their distance as he spoke.

"I mean none of you any harm and I am sorry about Raygan," he began.

"Raygan's ego took many lives," one wolf said stepping forward. "We are not okay with his death, but it would have come by your hand or another. It was only a question of time. We are here because we agree with the hybrid. Bloodshed is no longer necessary, as long as we respect each other."

"That will not be a problem," Casper eagerly confirmed.

"As to your relationship with Kylee," the wolf continued. "As long as it does not jeopardize our pack, you will be of no concern to us. Unless you do wrong by her, then you will have to answer to us."

The clearing of fifty plus men murmured their agreement and disappeared as swiftly as they had come. He turned to her and smiled.

"I hope you know that now means you are stuck with me for eternity and I come with brothers."

Ellie Scott

"Aarrggh," Kylee moaned. "The one called Aiden is annoying."

"That he is," Casper laughed, "but he means well."

"I know," she whispered.

He looked her in the eyes. "I love you Kylee, and I am looking forward to the adventures we have ahead of us."

Her only response was a promise of forever, sealed with a kiss.

Read on for an excerpt of Ellie Scott's newest paranormal novel *Evolution.*

Alpha vs. Vampire

Ellie Scott

Alpha vs. Vampire

EVOLUTION

EVOLUTION TRILOGY BOOK 1

By

ELLIE SCOTT

Copyright © 2016

Ellie Scott

PROLOGUE

I was never one for writing.

At the Institute, I was basically infamous for turning in my blank research reports. I was also once stuffed into the isolation chamber by an irate professor for that crime but it never bothered me.

I guess life never bothered me at the Institute. I was always curious what life was like in the realms. What I would be like when I changed. But until then, I was content going with the flow at the Institute, the only home I had ever known. My friends were my family. The hardest part of the change was the thought of not being around most of them again. Some people (most people that I have met) think about what they are going to do with their life after they change. I once asked someone how they knew what they are going to turn into and their answer was that they had always known from within.

I envied them.

Ellie Scott

But it was later I realized that it was that envy that
really crippled me in the end.

Alpha vs. Vampire

Ellie Scott

Part I

"In time the earth will be inhabited by almost god-like beings who shall analyze and discuss the remnants of humanity as we now discuss the chimpanzee."

Ella Wheeler Wilcox

Ellie Scott

CHAPTER ONE

They gave me pea soup again.

I wanted to protest, I almost did, but the look on Carly's face was enough for me. She stared me down, daring me to protest her ladling of pea soup into the metal bowl that was located on the right-hand corner of my tray. The bowl defied physics as Carly filled it with soup, refusing to fall over. The smell of it wasn't bad but in general, I wasn't a fan of soup that was green.

She didn't even put the dollop of sour cream that she usually did for everyone else; no I was exempt from that rule. Instead, she slipped in a piece of bread and handed me my spoon. Though her stare was terrifying, I had to say something.

"That's it?"

"Orders from above," she replied, making it sound as if it was some sort of secret thing.

I groaned and managed a half glare. I had been having the same pea soup for two days and it wasn't that it was bad, I just didn't like soup that looked green.

"I have been good," I said, trying to sound convincing.

Carly rolled her eyes. Her eyes were pale and the action made it seem like her pupil had melded with the background. Momentarily terrifying but not enough for me to cry out like a little girl. She raised her thin hands and touched the bracelet on her wrist. I looked down automatically on my own. The bracelet was silver with a small round jewel attached to it. Right now, the jewel was a bright green which I knew indicated that I was healthy.

"It's green," I said stubbornly.

"So is your soup," Carly said, grinning. "Don't try to fool them, they know what you need to eat."

I pouted but I knew there was no winning her over. Carly's grin widened and her cheekbones became prominent. She was easily twenty years older than me but looked older, perhaps because of the hours she had spent servicing the students and faculty of the Institute.

Alpha vs. Vampire

I grumbled under my breath and backed away from her, trying to make it look like I wasn't the defeated party but I don't think I was fooling anyone in that aspect. I turned around and scanned the hall for an empty table and spotted one in the corner. As I walked through the long tables, some people raised their hands and I acknowledged them with a half-smile. If I wanted, I could sit with them and talk to them but given my 'condition', that would bring about a lot of uncomfortable questions that I didn't want to answer right now.

Unfortunately, the table that I had chosen for myself was littered with wrappers and crumbs. I sighed and looked around vainly to see if there was another table that could be chosen but I was out of luck. I shouldn't have come here during lunch hour. Usually, I never did. I was one of those people who waited until lunch hour was almost over but today, Professor Kerrigan had forced me to go early. Her exact words had been,

"I don't want you to starve while you are at a delicate stage."

I reached into my pocket, drawing out a tissue and swept away the litter gingerly and sat down. The tray made some noise as it settled on the table but it was masked by the loudness of the hall.

Ellie Scott

I took up the spoon and dipped it into the steaming bowl of soup, blowing on it gently before putting it into my mouth. The taste made me grimace but I forced myself to swallow. Ugh, I really didn't like drinking soup.

The bread helped in clearing the taste from my mind but it was just bread, plain and tasteless. I craved something flavorful like pizza or pasta or anything but pea soup and bread. I glared at the bracelet on my wrist, they had been keeping a close eye on me ever since my 'condition' was confirmed.

It was unnecessary and truthfully, I couldn't really empathize with them about the situation. I wasn't dying, I was just pregnant.

From what everyone had told me, I expected the revelation to pack a punch but when I heard the news, I was as blank as I had been when Professor Johnson had announced that I had scored the lowest in my History class. I didn't really care about that or care about the child currently in me.

I may sound careless but there would be no good in lying to myself. The kid was there, it was a part of me and that's how it was going to remain. Forming an attachment to the kid would end up hurting me.

I was quite firm on that aspect but my heart did betray an ounce of sympathy for the child. It was expected but not something to worry about. I was more focused on how I was going to manage to finish my food. I continued to scarf it down when a shadow fell over me.

I looked up and there was Jenny, grinning down at me. Her short red hair was pulled back with a hairband and she was wearing a lab coat over her casual wear of a blue shirt and jeans. She had a tray with her but unlike mine, her tray had a burger with fries. My stomach growled as the smell of the meat wafted under my nose and I had to resist standing up to pull the tray away from her. She sat down next to me which made my self-control waver even further.

I tore my eyes away from it and focused on her freckled face.

"Lab?"

"We did cool stuff today," Jenny said. "I actually got to watch a cell mutate."

My eyes kept sliding down and it took all my concentration to look at Jenny. "That sounds great."

"It was, did you know that it multiplies at thrice the rate that normal cell division occurs?"

"I am sure I heard that somewhere."

"You should have taken the class with me."

89

Ellie Scott

"I don't have the patience for it."

"You don't have the patience for anything, not even the bowl of soup you have," Jenny said.

"It's almost done," I said defensively. My spoon had made contact with the bottom of the bowl and defiantly, I picked it up and drained it.

Jenny smiled like a mom who knew that her child was stupid but still loved the child anyway.   I stuffed the last bit of bread into my mouth and almost choked from the dry texture. Jenny had my back, sliding across her bottle of water. I unscrewed it and took a long gulp, before sighing.

"Thanks," I said.

"No problem. Want some French fries?"

I smiled easily at that sentence and picked up two of them, popping them into my mouth and chewing contently. Jenny smiled and dug into her hamburger.

"So how do you feel?"

"Pretty much the same" I said, reaching for one more. Jenny didn't protest and I pushed my luck, picking up four more. Well, I am a monster when it comes to fries. In my opinion, food is the best thing that we brought from the Old ages. Everything differs in the other cities but here at the Institute, you get to have whatever you want and I have a fondness for the worst things possible.

"So…" Jenny stopped and looked at me.

"You can say what you want to say," I said.

"Have you talked to Jeremy?"

I stopped in the middle of popping a French fry in my mouth. Awkward questions weren't good for your mental health and I tried to pretend I was okay by going back to eating.

"Why would I talk to him?"

"Because he…"

"is the father of my child?" I finished her sentence and gave her a hard look.

Jenny blushed slightly and said, "You know that you have to talk to him at one point."

"Did you talk to Stan when you were pregnant?"

"Yes, I did."

I bit my lip, she had ruined my comeback. I was so sure that she had not that the retort had been on the tip of my tongue. I swallowed it back and said,

Ellie Scott

"Well, you and I are not the same."

I knew that Jenny had a point, a really good point. I should talk to Jeremy if only to preserve our friendship. Jeremy, Jenny and I have been friends from the time we were kids. We were always together, which isn't all that hard when you are stuck inside the Institute but you get the point. The point is, we are really good friends. That was until the higher ups decided that Jeremy was the best match for me.

Okay, I think I have to start from the beginning if only to make some sense.

The world is different. In this world, humans exist until they turn 18. After that, they become something else. They either become a werewolf, vampire, demon or witch/warlock. When the change happens, they are sent to cities where they live out their lives among their kind.

Because the population would be screwed if it could not reproduce, humans from the Institute are required to give birth at least once before they turn 18. The babies are taken and housed at another extension of the Institute where the cycle continues.

We need it for survival and besides, we aren't really required to do anything. The higher ups choose the perfect genetic match for us and then they perform in-vitro fertilization. Once pregnant, you are incubated at a certain point and the pregnancy is accelerated.

Alpha vs. Vampire

Not exactly like how it used to go in the old world but I didn't have much choice in the matter.

Basically, Jeremy was my perfect genetic match which made things awkward between us, but I think what made it even more awkward was my inability to admit that I liked him a lot. Maybe even more than a friend. Yeah, I took the awkwardness thing to a whole new level.

So ever since it was confirmed that I was pregnant, I have been avoiding it. In my mind, this was only because of the baby. Soon it would be alright and we would go back to normal or at least I hoped that would happen.

"After the baby comes," I said firmly to Jenny.

"That's like four weeks!" Jenny exclaimed.

"How are you so sure?"

Jenny flushed. "I am estimating. I have been through this."

"I haven't reached that point yet."

Now here's the thing, I like being right but apparently, karma doesn't like that because as I finished that sentence, my bracelet began to glow red. Jenny noticed it and looked up.

Ellie Scott

"Sasha, you are—"

She didn't get to finish that sentence. Three men burst through the doors and headed directly for me. My instinct was to run but I controlled myself. This was expected. This was normal. That didn't stop the rush of fear as their hands closed on me.

"Sasha Peterson, it's time to come with us."

For your copy of Evolution, please click <u>here.</u>

Alpha vs. Vampire

Ellie Scott

ABOUT THE AUTHOR

Ellie Scott

Ellie has her degree in Clinical Psychology, but after years studying deviant behavior, decided to devote her skills to developing stories that twist reality. Her favorite genres are medical mystery and anything in the paranormal world. Ellie writes full time in her home in South Carolina that she shares with her husband and two toy poodles.

Find out more on Facebook or on Amazon at Ellie Scott.

Ellie Scott

OTHER BOOKS BY ELLIE SCOTT

Now available on Amazon- Evolution- the first in a trilogy that follows a young woman turning eighteen and not mutating as she should be. Is her deviant biology a threat to the realms of the new world?

The first in the Vampire Reclaiming series introduces us to Jack and Maya. Jack is back in town he helped build after a long absence and not welcomed by the wolves, who aren't your typical shifter. As Jack is drawn to Maya, danger surrounds them as the alpha wolf wants Jack gone.

Check out the first book in the Camille Carter Mystery Series: Too Close to Home: A Camille Carter Novel. Camille is about to graduate from her master's program, but a discovery of wrong doing by her mentor and would be suitor puts that in jeopardy.

Too Far From Home, the second Camille Carter Novel, follows Camille as she is on her first CDC mission in Nigeria trying to solve why children are getting sick and dying in the rural community.

Ellie Scott

Alpha vs. Vampire

<u>The Weak Can't Survive: The Haunting of Mount Vruul</u> is a story about a teen who comes face to face with her fears on a holiday in the mountains.

Ellie Scott

AUTHOR NOTE

If you enjoyed this book, found it useful or otherwise then I'd really appreciate it if you would post a short review on Amazon. I do read all the reviews personally so that I can continually write what people are wanting.

Thanks for your support!

Ellie Scott

19979556R00063

Printed in Great Britain
by Amazon